Art Works™ Drawing fairies and Mermaids

Carolyn Scrace

SCRIBBLERS

D0231456

Author:
Carolyn Scrace graduated from Brighton College of Art, UK, with a focus on design and illustration. She has since worked in animation, advertising and children's publishing. She has a special interest in natural history and has written many books on the subject, including *Lion Journal* and *Gorilla Journal* in the *Animal Journal* series.

How to use this book:

Follow the easy, numbered instructions. Simple step-by-step stages enable budding young artists to create their own amazing drawings.

What you will need:

1. Paper.
2. Wax crayons.
3. Felt-tip pens to add colour.

Published in Great Britain in MMXV by Scribblers, a division of Book House
25 Marlborough Place, Brighton BN1 1UB
www.salariya.com
www.book-house.co.uk

ISBN-13: 978-1-910184-83-7

1 3 5 7 9 8 6 4 2

A CIP catalogue record for this book is available from the British Library.

Printed and bound in China.

Contents

Fairy Bluebell

1 Fairy Bluebell needs a head,

2 ...a flower-shaped body,

3 ...two legs and feet,

4 ...two arms and hands,

5 ...and two **big** wings!

6 Draw in her hair and two pointed ears!

Crayon in spots on Bluebell's wings.

Draw in her eyes, nose, mouth and rosy cheeks.

Add Bluebell's fairy wand!

Colour in with felt-tip pens.

5

Fairy Daisy

1 Daisy needs a head,

2 ...a body,

3 ...two legs and feet,

4 ...and two arms and hands.

5 Now draw in her wings and ears!

6 Add a skirt made of **petals**.

Draw in Daisy's fringe with petals round her head!

Add her eyes, nose and mouth.

Draw in Daisy's fairy wand.

Colour in with felt-tip pens.

7

Fairy Poppy

1 Poppy needs a head,

2 ...a body,

3 ...a skirt made from flower petals,

4 ...two legs and feet,

5 ...and two arms, hands and wings.

6 Now crayon in her long, wavy hair.

Add Poppy's fairy wand!

Draw in her eyes, nose, mouth and two rosy cheeks!

Colour in with felt-tip pens.

Fairy Acorn

1 Acorn needs a head,

2 ...a **zigzag** body,

3 ... a pair of shorts, two legs and feet,

4 ...two arms and hands,

5 ...and his two wings!

6 Now draw in his pointed ears and acorn-shaped hat!

Crayon in a pattern
of squares on his
acorn-shaped hat.

Add Acorn's
fairy wand!

Draw in his eyes,
nose, mouth and
two pink cheeks!

Colour in with
felt-tip pens.

11

Fairy Buttercup

1 Buttercup needs a head,

2 ...a body,

3 ...a **frilly** skirt,

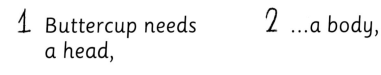

4 ...two legs and feet,

5 ...and two arms and hands.

6 Add two wings and a pointed ear!

Draw in her hair with some flowers.

Add Buttercup's eyes, nose and mouth.

Draw in her fairy wand.

Colour in with felt-tip pens.

13

Fairy Lily

1 Lily needs a head,

2 ...a body and a petal-shaped skirt,

3 ...two legs and feet,

4 ...two arms and hands,

5 ...and two wings.

6 Now draw in a **very big** lily-shaped hat!

Draw in her eyes, nose, mouth and rosy cheeks!

Draw in Lily's hair.

Crayon in spots over her body.

Draw in her fairy wand.

Colour in with felt-tip pens.

Fairy Leaf

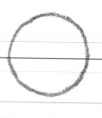

1 Leaf needs a head,

2 ...a body,

3 ...a pair of shorts,
two legs and feet,

3 ...two arms
and hands,

5 ...and two wings.

6 Now draw in one
ear and add his
curly hair.

16

Draw in Leaf's eyes, nose and mouth.

Draw in his fairy wand.

Add crayon lines to make his wings look like leaves.

Colour in with felt-tip pens.

17

Mermaid Shelly

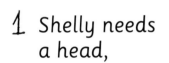
Tail fin

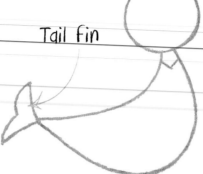

1 Shelly needs a head,

2 ...a body and a tail fin,

3 ...two arms and hands,

4 ... and **very long**, curly hair.

5 To make the fish-scale pattern: draw lines in one direction,

6 ...then add rows of lines in the opposite direction.

18

Crayon in tiny shells
to decorate her hair.

Draw in Shelly's eyes,
nose, mouth and two
rosy cheeks!

Colour in with
felt-tip pens.

19

Mermaid Pearl

Tail fin

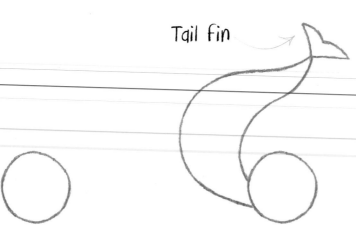

1 Pearl needs a head,

2 ...a body and a tail fin,

3 ...two arms and hands,

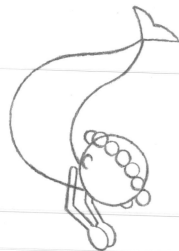

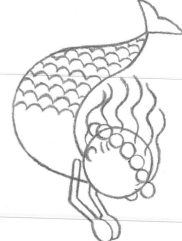

4 ...two ears and a **pearl** headband,

5 ...and long curly hair.

6 Draw in the wavy pattern of her scales.

20

Colour in with felt-tip pens.

Draw in Pearl's eyes, nose and mouth.

21

Mermaid Star

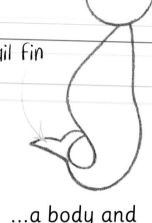

Tail fin

1 Star needs a head,

2 ...a body and a tail fin,

3 ...two arms and hands,

4 ...long, flowing hair,

5 ...a **star** in her hair and a matching pendant.

6 Now draw the pattern of her scales!

Draw in Star's eyes, nose and mouth.

Colour in with *felt-tip pens.*

23

Mermaid Coral

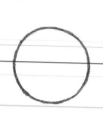

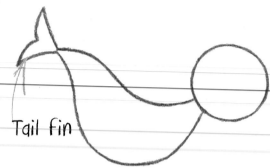

Tail fin

1 Coral needs a head,

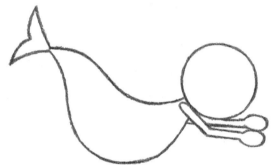

2 ...a body and a tail fin,

3 ...two arms and hands,

4 ...two ears and **very** curly hair.

5 To make a fish-scale pattern: draw lines in one direction,

6 ...then add rows of lines in the opposite direction.

Draw in Coral's eyes, nose and mouth.

Add some shells and a starfish to decorate her hair.

Colour in with felt-tip pens.

25

Mermaid Marina

Tail fin

1 Marina needs a head,

2 ...a body and a tail fin,

3 ...two arms and hands,

4 ...two ears and long, wavy hair.

5 Draw in the fish-scale pattern.

6 Add her eyes, nose and mouth.

Crayon in some **pretty seaweed** on Marina's hair.

Colour in with felt-tip pens.

27

Mermaid Breeze

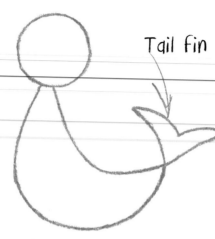

Tail fin

1 Breeze needs a head,

2 ...a body and a tail fin,

3 ...two arms and hands,

4 ...one ear and curly hair.

5 Now draw in the pattern of scales,

6 ...and her eyes, nose and mouth.

Crayon in a
starfish
on her hair.

Draw in Breeze's
shell trumpet!

Colour in with
felt-tip pens.

Mermaid Misty

Tail fin

1 Misty needs a head,

2 ...a body and a tail fin,

3 ...and two ears, two arms and hands!

4 Now draw five seashells round the top of her head,

5 ...and add long **flowing** hair.

6 Crayon in the pattern of her scales.

Colour in with felt-tip pens.

Crayon in spots on Misty's tail fin.

Draw in Misty's eyes, nose and mouth.

31

glossary

Acorn a smooth nut in a cup-shaped holder, the fruit of an oak tree.

Fairy a tiny imaginary being in human form, with magical powers.

Mermaid an imaginary sea creature, half woman and half fish.

Pattern a repeated shape or design used to decorate something.

Pearl a smooth, round jewel formed inside an oyster or clam shell.

Scale a flat plate forming part of the body covering of fish and other animals.

Seaweed a plant that grows in the sea. You will often find it washed up on beaches.

Starfish a sea creature, usually with five arms, that feeds on shellfish.

Tail fin a fin at the rear end of a fish, whale, etc.

index